EFT Tapping Therapy

The Comprehensive Guide For Mastering
Emotional Freedom Techniques and
Overcoming Anxiety, Healing Trauma, and
Cultivating Resilience.

Title:
EFT Tapping Therapy

Subtitle

The Comprehensive Guide For Mastering Emotional Freedom Techniques and Overcoming Anxiety, Healing Trauma, and Cultivating Resilience.

Copyright © 2024 by (Dr. Jodie Stamm)

Printed in the United States of America.

ISBN: 9798883243881

TABLE OF CONTENT

INTRODUCTION

As a result of the fast-paced society in which we currently reside, where stresses are abundant and mental health difficulties are on the rise, individuals are consistently looking for effective techniques to reduce emotional discomfort, overcome previous traumas, and enhance their overall well-being. In recent years, Emotional Freedom Techniques (EFT) Tapping Therapy has emerged as a method that has garnered a considerable amount of attention and popularity. To provide a full understanding of EFT Tapping Therapy, this introduction will cover topics such as its definition, history, origins, and the underlying processes that are responsible for its effectiveness.

UNDERSTANDING EFT TAPPING THERAPY

At its foundation, EFT Tapping Therapy is a holistic healing approach that addresses emotional, physical, and psychological difficulties by combining components of traditional Chinese medicine, psychology, and modern psychotherapy. This modality is commonly referred to as EFT Tapping Therapy. Acupressure is a method that includes tapping on certain acupressure sites on the body while concentrating on particular ideas, feelings, or memories. In this way, individuals strive to free themselves from negative energy blockages and bring the energy system of the body back into balance, which ultimately leads to the promotion of emotional healing and overall well-being.

What is EFT?

Since emotional freedom techniques (EFT) resemble acupuncture but don't involve needles, they're also referred to as "psychological acupressure." Rather than utilizing needles, practitioners verbalize affirmations or concentrate on particular concerns while tapping on important meridian points on the body with their fingertips. It is said that by gently tapping the body, emotional blockages are released and the body's energy flow is stimulated, resulting in a feeling of emotional relief and liberation.

The idea of "thought field treatment," which holds that painful memories and unpleasant emotions are stored in the body's energy system and may be effectively addressed by tapping on particular areas while tuning into the related thoughts and feelings, is one of the fundamental tenets of EFT. People can interrupt their negative thought patterns and let go of the emotional baggage related to previous traumas or present pressures by tapping on these locations.

History and Origins

Since emotional freedom techniques (EFT) resemble acupuncture but don't involve needles, they're also referred to as "psychological acupressure." Rather than utilizing needles, practitioners verbalize affirmations or concentrate on particular concerns while tapping on important meridian points on the body with their fingertips. It is said that by gently tapping the body, emotional blockages are released and the body's energy flow is stimulated, resulting in a feeling of emotional relief and liberation.

The idea of "thought field treatment," which holds that painful memories and unpleasant emotions are stored in the body's energy system and may be effectively addressed by tapping on particular areas while tuning into the related thoughts and feelings, is one of the fundamental tenets of EFT. People can interrupt their negative thought patterns and let go of the emotional baggage related to previous traumas or present pressures by tapping on these locations.

How EFT Works

There is still much to learn and discuss about the fundamental mechanics behind EFT. Nonetheless, several hypotheses have been put out to explain why it works so effectively in fostering emotional recovery and wellbeing.

The idea of the body's energy system as it is perceived in traditional Chinese medicine is one of the fundamental tenets of EFT. This viewpoint holds that vital energy, or Qi, runs along a network of meridians, or energy channels, that cross the body. This energy flow can become obstructed or disturbed, resulting in emotional or physical problems. EFT is said to release these energy blockages and bring the body's energy system back into balance by tapping on particular acupressure points, which reduce symptoms and speed up healing.

Furthermore, it is believed that EFT activates the stress response system of the body, particularly the amygdala, which is crucial for processing emotions and initiating the fight-or-flight response. EFT is supposed to deliver soothing signals to the amygdala by having practitioners tap on certain areas while tuning into disturbing thoughts or emotions. This lessens the intensity of the emotional reaction and fosters a sense of well-being and relaxation.

Moreover, exposure therapy and cognitive restructuring two well-known therapeutic modalities for treating anxiety and trauma-related disorders are incorporated into EFT. People are encouraged to face and reframe unwanted thoughts or memories by verbally stating affirmations or phrases about the topic at hand while tapping on certain areas. This results in a shift in perspective and emotional healing.

PART I: GETTING STARTED WITH EFT TAPPING

THE BASICS OF EFT TAPPING

Tap therapy, which is part of the Emotional Freedom Techniques (EFT) approach, is a straightforward yet effective way of resolving a wide range of concerns, including emotional anguish, physical discomfort, and many other problems. Emotional Freedom Technique (EFT) tapping is a technique that includes pressing certain acupressure points on the body while concentrating on specific thoughts, feelings, or memories. This section looks into the fundamental features of EFT tapping, including tapping points, providing instructions on how to do EFT tapping, and highlighting the need to develop a routine to get the best possible outcomes.

The Tapping Points

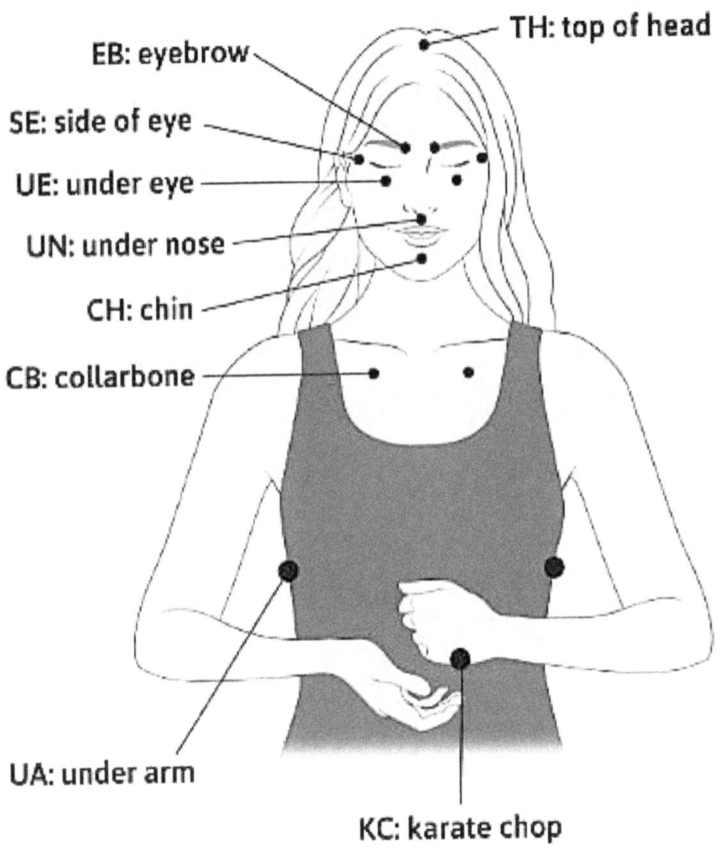

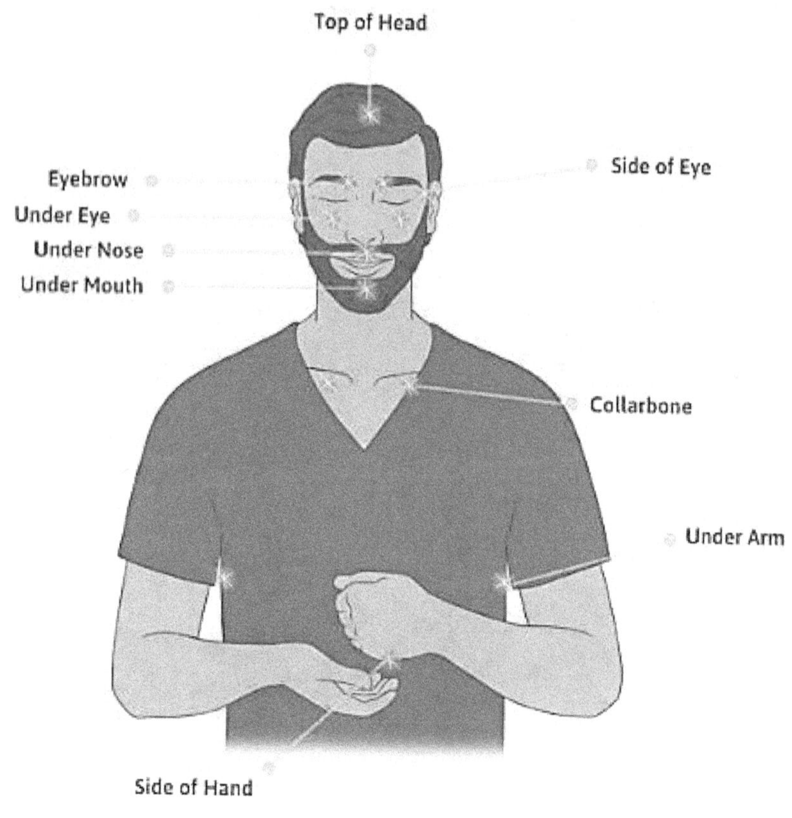

The body's meridian system has several particular acupressure sites that are used in EFT tapping. It is thought that these points correlate to various energy channels, bodily experiences, and emotions. People try to clear energy blockages and bring the body's energy system back into balance by tapping on these locations. The main EFT tapping points are as follows:

- **Karate Chop Point (KC):** situated between the wrist and the base of the pinky finger on the hand's fleshy outer border. This stage is frequently utilized for the EFT setup statement, in which participants express their vocal affirmation or recognition of the problem that has to be solved.

- **Top of the Head (TH):** situated in the middle, at the top of the head. It is said that tapping on this area can reduce mental tension and encourage mental clarity.

- **Eyebrow (EB):** situated next to the nasal bridge, at the start of the eyebrow. It is believed that tapping on this area can reduce tension in the body and encourage emotional equilibrium.

- **Side of the Eye (SE):** situated near the outer corner of the eye on the bony ridge. It is said that tapping on this location might help you relax and let go of bad feelings.

- **Under the Eye (UE):** situated about an inch below the pupil on the bone behind the eye. It is believed that tapping on this area can reduce tension and encourage serenity.

- **Under the Nose (UN):** situated in the groove created by the nose and upper lip. It is said that tapping on this area relieves stress and encourages emotional stability.

- **Chin (CH):** situated in the furrow that separates the chin from the lower lip. It is said that tapping on this spot might help to heal emotionally by releasing emotional barriers.

- **Collarbone (CB):** situated where it joins the breastbone, directly below the collarbone. It is said that tapping on this area can help to regulate emotions and relieve energy blockages.

- **Under the Arm (UA):** situated down the side of the body, about four inches below the armpit. It is said that tapping on this area would reduce stress and encourage calmness.

- **Wrists (WR):** There are situations where EFT tapping sequences include tapping on the inside of the wrists. It is said that this area encourages emotional discharge and calm.

How to Perform EFT Tapping

Anybody, regardless of age or skill level, may perform EFT tapping because it is a fairly easy process. Here's how to execute EFT tapping step-by-step:

- Identify the Issue: Decide exactly what problem or feeling you want to use EFT tapping to resolve first. This might be anything from physical discomfort or limiting beliefs to worry and stress.

- Rate the Intensity: Before initiating the tapping sequence, assign a number to the issue's intensity (0 being no intensity and 10 being the greatest feasible). This will enable you to monitor your development during the tapping session.

- The Setup Statement: Create a setup statement that first identifies the problem and then affirms your unconditional love and acceptance of yourself. For example "Even though I feel anxious, I deeply and completely accept myself."

- Tap the Karate Chop Point: Repeat the setup statement three times while lightly tapping the karate chop spot on the other hand with the fingers of one hand.

- Tap the Remaining Points: Tap on each of the remaining tapping spots according to the previously mentioned order. Keep your attention on the problem or feeling you are trying to solve while you touch on each spot. If it feels right, you can speak affirmations or remarks about the problem aloud.

- Repeat the Sequence: For two or three rounds, or as many times as necessary, repeat the tapping process until you notice a change in your emotional state or a reduction in the severity of the problem.

- Check the Intensity: Once you have finished the tapping sequence, rate the issue's intensity again from 0 to 10. Ideally, you should experience a change in your emotional state or a decrease in intensity.

- Closure: Take a few deep breaths, confirm your self-acceptance, and state that you are prepared to let go of the issue to wrap up the tapping session. Additionally, you might repeat a closing sentence or a good affirmation while tapping on the karate chop spot one more.

Establishing a Routine

Even though EFT tapping might be useful on its own, developing a regular tapping practice can maximize its advantages and support long-term emotional health. The following advice will help you create a productive EFT tapping schedule:

1. Set Aside Time: Establish regular timeslots, ideally once or twice a day, for EFT tapping sessions. The secret to optimizing the advantages of tapping is consistency.

2. Choose a Quiet Environment: Locate a peaceful, cozy area where you may practice EFT tapping without interruptions. This might be a calm outside environment or a quiet space in your house.

3. Start Small: If you've never used EFT tapping before, begin with five to ten-minute tapping sessions and work your way up to longer sessions as you get more experience.

4. Focus on Specific Issues: Customize your tapping sessions to target particular problems or feelings you're going through right now. This might involve physical discomfort, worry, anxiety, or restricting beliefs.

5. Track Your Progress: To monitor your development and record any adjustments to your physical or mental symptoms, keep a diary. This might assist you in seeing trends and tracking how well your tapping regimen is working.

6. Stay Open-Minded: Be receptive to learning about the possible advantages of EFT tapping and approach it with an open mind. Even while the method can appear strange at first, with regular practice, many people have reported significant improvements.

You may optimize the efficacy of the method and enjoy greater emotional freedom and well-being over time by implementing these concepts into your EFT tapping regimen. This will allow you to maximize the effectiveness of the procedure.

ADDRESSING EMOTIONAL BLOCKS

Emotional blockages are obstacles that restrict people from completely feeling and expressing their feelings. These obstacles may result from unresolved emotional problems, cultural indoctrination, bad attitudes, or traumatic experiences in the past. Emotional Freedom Techniques (EFT) tapping provides a potent method to recognize, release, and transcend emotional obstacles, which are an essential part of emotional healing and personal development. This thorough investigation will focus on the steps involved in resolving emotional obstacles, such as recognizing them, letting go of unpleasant feelings, and getting over resistance.

Identifying Emotional Blocks

Effectively overcoming emotional obstacles begins with identifying them. Emotional obstacles can take many different forms, such as self-doubt, guilt, shame, rage, fear, or worry. These obstacles might be brought on by painful experiences in the past, unfavorable views about oneself or the outside world, or ingrained behavioral habits.

Self-awareness and introspection are two tools that may be used to detect emotional barriers. Understanding underlying emotional barriers may be gained by keeping an eye on your thoughts, feelings, and behavioral patterns. Introspective techniques like mindfulness meditation, counseling, and journaling can also help identify emotional boundaries that may be buried.

Common signs of emotional blocks include:

- Avoidance refers to avoiding specific events, activities, or people out of fear or discomfort.

- Self-sabotage is defined as engaging in self-destructive actions or practices that undermine one's well-being and achievement.

- Procrastination: Delaying important activities or choices due to fear or uncertainty.

- Emotional Reactivity: An impulsive or excessive reaction to stimuli or triggers.

- Physical Symptoms: Emotional stress can cause physical symptoms such as tension, headaches, or gastrointestinal difficulties.

- Low self-esteem refers to having a bad self-image or believing that one is undeserving of affection and acceptance.

By identifying these indications and paying attention to your internal feelings, you may start to uncover the emotional barriers that may be preventing you from living a meaningful and genuine life.

Releasing Negative Emotions

Once you've discovered emotional obstacles, the next step is to remove the unpleasant feelings that come with them. EFT tapping is a highly effective method for releasing negative emotions and restoring emotional equilibrium. The tapping technique works by activating certain acupressure points on the body while focusing on the emotional issue or memory in question.

Here's a step-by-step procedure for releasing unpleasant emotions with EFT tapping:

- **Identify the Emotion:** Determine the precise unpleasant feeling you wish to address first. This might include feelings of shame, guilt, rage, or fear.

- **Rate the Intensity:** On a scale of 0 to 10, where 10 represents the maximum intensity imaginable, rate the emotion's intensity. This will enable you to monitor your development during the tapping session.

- **Formulate the Setup Statement:** Write a setup statement that affirms unconditional love and self-acceptance while acknowledging the unpleasant feeling. "Even if I feel [emotion], I profoundly and embrace myself," for instance, is one example.

- **Tap the Karate Chop Point:** Repeat the setup statement three times while lightly tapping the karate chop spot on the other hand with the fingers of one hand.

- **Tap the Remaining Points:** As you continue, make remarks about the negative feeling and touch on each of the remaining tapping spots in the previously described order. Sayings like "I chose to release this [emotion]," "This [emotion] is unpleasant," or "I feel [emotion] in my body" are examples.

- **Repeat the Sequence:** After two or three rounds, or as many times as necessary, repeat the tapping process until you notice a change in your emotional state or a reduction in the intensity of the feeling.

- **Check the Intensity:** Once you have finished the tapping pattern, rate the emotion again from 0 to 10. Ideally, you should experience a change in your emotional state or a decrease in intensity.

- **Closure:** Take a few deep breaths, confirm your self-acceptance, and express your readiness to let go of the unpleasant feeling to wrap up the tapping session. Additionally, you might repeat a closing sentence or a good affirmation while tapping on the karate chop spot one more.

You may gradually remove emotional obstacles and feel greater emotional freedom and well-being if you continuously practice EFT tapping to release negative emotions. This can be accomplished by tapping on your ears.

Overcoming Resistance

When attempting to overcome emotional barriers, one of the most typical obstacles that may appear is resistance. It is possible for resistance to take the form of an unwillingness to address difficult emotions, a fear of change, or a mistrust over the efficacy of EFT tapping. Having compassion, tolerance, and perseverance are all necessary components in overcoming opposition.

As part of the process of resolving emotional barriers, the following are some tactics that may be utilized to overcome resistance:

- Cultivate Self-Compassion: Be kind and patient with yourself while you work through challenging feelings. Acknowledge that recovery takes time and that it's acceptable to have discomfort or uncertainty while going through it.

- Challenge Limiting Beliefs: Determine whether negative self-talk or limiting ideas are causing resistance, then address and overcome them. Affirmations of empowerment and encouraging self-statements should take the place of these beliefs.

- Take Small Steps: Divide overcoming emotional obstacles into smaller, more doable actions. Rather than attempting to handle everything at once, concentrate on making little, consistent progress.

- Seek Support: Seek assistance and direction from dependable family members, friends, or mental health specialists. Talking to others about your experiences can provide you with perspective, encouragement, and affirmation.

- Practice Mindfulness: Develop present-moment awareness and mindfulness to perceive resistance without passing judgment. When resistance emerges, pay attention to any thoughts, emotions, or bodily sensations that come up; then, let them pass without becoming sucked into them.

- Celebrate Progress: No matter how tiny, acknowledge and applaud your success. You may achieve more emotional freedom and wellbeing with each action you take to overcome emotional blockages.

You will be able to progressively overcome obstacles and go on a road of emotional healing and personal development if you face opposition with compassion, patience, and tenacity.

PART II: APPLYING EFT TAPPING THERAPY

EFT FOR STRESS AND ANXIETY

People of all ages and from all walks of life are affected by the issues of stress and anxiety, which have grown increasingly ubiquitous in modern life. However, prolonged stress and anxiety can have substantial effects on both mental and physical health, even though experiencing stress on occasion is a natural and expected part of life. To our good fortune, Emotional Freedom Techniques (EFT) provides a strong and efficient method for the management of stress and anxiety. This in-depth investigation will look into the use of EFT for the management of stress and anxiety, including, but not limited to, the management of everyday stress, the conquering of anxiety disorders, and the management of panic attacks.

Managing Everyday Stress

Daily stresses that can negatively impact mental and emotional health include financial strains, marital problems, work demands, and hectic schedules. To be balanced and resilient in the face of adversity, one must learn to manage daily stress. EFT tapping is a straightforward yet powerful approach for lowering stress and encouraging calm.

The following are some strategies for using EFT to handle daily stress:

Identify Triggers: To begin, pinpoint the precise circumstances, ideas, or occurrences that set off stress reactions. This might involve anxieties about money, disagreements with family members or coworkers, or deadlines at work.

Create Tapping Scripts: Once you've discovered your stress triggers, write tapping scripts to handle them specifically. Create setup statements that identify the stressor and affirm self-acceptance and relaxation. For example, "Even if I am anxious about [a certain scenario], I sincerely accept myself and choose to relax."

Practice Regularly: Set aside some time each day to practice EFT tapping for stress reduction. You may add tapping into your morning or evening routines, or utilize it whenever you're anxious or overwhelmed.

Focus on the Body: While tapping, pay attention to your body's physical sensations of stress and tension. Identify regions of tension or discomfort and tap on the associated acupressure points while saying affirmations of relaxation and release.

Use Positive Affirmations: Include uplifting statements in your tapping scripts to help you feel more at ease, resilient, and confident. Recite affirmations like "I choose to let go of tension and embrace tranquility," "I am calm and centered," and "I trust in my abilities to face obstacles" aloud.

Through the integration of EFT tapping into your everyday schedule and proactive management of stressors, you may lower your stress threshold, boost your resilience, and develop a deeper feeling of inner tranquility and overall wellbeing.

Overcoming Anxiety Disorders

Excessive and ongoing worry, fear, or uneasiness that can impair everyday functioning and quality of life are the hallmarks of anxiety disorders. Panic disorder, phobias, social anxiety disorder, and generalized anxiety disorder (GAD) are examples of common anxiety disorders. Even though anxiety problems may be quite crippling, EFT tapping is a viable method for lessening anxiety symptoms and regaining emotional equilibrium.

The following are some strategies for using EFT to treat anxiety disorders:

Determine Underlying Beliefs: Examine the ideas and preconceptions that underlie anxious symptoms. Fears of failure, perfectionism, uncertainty, or negative self-talk are a few examples of these beliefs. To confront and reframe these limiting ideas, use EFT tapping.

Target Particular Symptoms: Modify your tapping scripts to specifically address particular anxiety symptoms or causes. If you are socially anxious, for instance, write tapping scripts that address your anxieties of being judged, rejected, or embarrassed in public.

- Practice Exposure Therapy: Gradually expose yourself to triggers or fearful circumstances by using EFT tapping in addition to exposure therapy approaches. Tapping to lessen anxiety symptoms might help you step up to more anxiety-provoking circumstances gradually from less difficult ones.

- Examine any prior traumas or events that could be influencing your anxiety symptoms. Address Trauma and Past Experiences. To facilitate healing and resolution, use EFT tapping to process and release emotional discomfort related to these previous occurrences.

- Incorporate Relaxation Techniques: To maximize the soothing benefits of EFT tapping and encourage relaxation, combine it with other relaxation techniques like progressive muscle relaxation, deep breathing, or visualization.

- Seek Professional Assistance: If you're having trouble controlling your anxiety symptoms on your own, you might want to consult with a mental health practitioner who has experience treating anxiety disorders with evidence-based therapies like EFT.

You may lessen the symptoms of anxiety, build self-awareness, and regain control over your thoughts and feelings by integrating EFT tapping into your anxiety management plan and addressing underlying beliefs and triggers.

Coping with Panic Attacks

Attacks of panic are abrupt periods of acute anxiety or discomfort that can be accompanied by physical symptoms such as heart palpitations, sweating, shaking, shortness of breath, and dizziness. Panic attacks can also be accompanied by a combination of these symptoms. The process of coping with panic attacks can be difficult, but EFT tapping is a helpful technique that can be used to manage panic symptoms and promote a sense of peace and control.

Utilizing EFT tapping, the following are some ways that may be utilized to manage panic attacks:

Learn to Detect Early Warning Signals It is important to learn how to recognize the early warning signs of a panic attack, which include a fast heartbeat, shortness of breath, or thoughts of impending doom. These indications should be used as signs to start tapping as soon as possible to prevent the panic attack from becoming more severe.

It is recommended that you incorporate grounding methods into your tapping practice. These techniques will assist you in establishing a sense of anchoring in the present now and will also help lessen feelings of dissociation or confusion. Focusing on your breath, employing sensory anchors like touch or sight, or repeating soothing mantras are all examples of practices that may be used to help you become more grounded.

When you tap on particular symptoms: Applying EFT tapping to particular panic symptoms, such as chest tightness, racing thoughts, or difficulty breathing, can help alleviate these symptoms. You should modify your tapping scripts such that they effectively address these symptoms while simultaneously confirming feelings of safety, relaxation, and self-assurance.

To witness panic symptoms without passing judgment or putting up resistance, it is important to cultivate mindfulness and present-moment awareness via practice. If you are experiencing panic episodes, you can use EFT tapping to access feelings of acceptance, compassion, and self-soothing.

A Panic Plan Should Be Created: Create a tailored panic plan that covers coping tactics, relaxation techniques, and support resources that may be utilized during panic episodes. To get instant relief and better control of symptoms, use EFT tapping as a core component of your approach for dealing with panic.

Seek the Assistance of Professionals: If you suffer from panic attacks that are severe or occur frequently, you must seek the assistance of a mental health professional who can offer you direction, support, and treatments that are supported by evidence, such as cognitive-behavioral therapy (CBT) or exposure therapy.

By including EFT tapping into your arsenal for managing panic attacks and proactively addressing panic symptoms, you may lessen the frequency and intensity of panic attacks, boost feelings of control and empowerment, and improve the overall quality of your life.

EFT FOR PHYSICAL PAIN

Physical discomfort is a common, sometimes incapacitating sensation that can negatively impact many facets of everyday life, including relationships, employment, and general well-being. Emotional Freedom Techniques (EFT) offer a supplemental approach that tackles the emotional and energetic elements of pain in addition to traditional therapies like medicine and physical therapy that help relieve physical pain. This thorough investigation will focus on using EFT to treat physical pain, such as chronic pain, migraines, and headaches, as well as reducing tension in the muscles.

Relieving Chronic Pain

Millions of individuals worldwide suffer from chronic pain, which is defined as continuous pain that lasts longer than three months. Chronic pain can significantly lower the quality of life. Often, managing chronic pain requires a multidisciplinary strategy that takes into account psychological, emotional, and physical aspects. To treat the emotional and energetic aspects of chronic pain, EFT tapping offers a special and useful technique that can lower pain levels and enhance general wellbeing.

The following are some methods for using EFT to treat persistent pain:

Determine Pain Triggers: To begin with, determine which patterns or triggers in particular make your chronic pain worse. These triggers might be specific behaviors, settings, feelings, or ideas that exacerbate pain sensations.

Address Emotional Elements: Stress, anxiety, despair, and traumatic experiences are some of the emotional factors that are frequently linked to chronic pain. For increased relaxation and pain reduction, use EFT tapping to treat and release emotional discomfort linked to chronic pain.

Target Pain Symptoms: Customize your tapping scripts to focus on particular bodily pains or sore spots. To help with alleviation, tap on acupressure points like the top of the head or the side of the hand (also known as the "karate chop point") and concentrate on describing the pain sensations in detail.

Practice Mind-Body Methods: To improve relaxation and pain management, combine EFT tapping with mind-body methods like progressive muscle relaxation, guided imagery, or deep breathing. Make use of these methods to ease tension in your muscles and encourage a state of tranquility throughout your body.

Address Limiting Views: Examine any self-talk that perpetuates negative beliefs about chronic pain, such as powerlessness, worthlessness, or hopelessness. Replace these ideas with powerful statements of healing and resilience by using EFT tapping to confront and reframe them.

EFT tapping can help you manage chronic pain by treating its emotional and energy roots. This can help you feel less pain, feel more relaxed, and live a better overall life.

Alleviating Headaches and Migraines

Common pain kinds that can vary from little discomfort to severe debilitation include headaches and migraines. Although taking medication might temporarily relieve headache symptoms, it is important to note that drugs frequently have adverse effects and may not address the underlying reasons for headaches. By treating the mental and physical components of pain, EFT tapping provides a safe, all-natural method of treating headaches and migraines.

The following are some methods for using EFT to treat migraines and headaches:

Determine Triggers: The first step in treating your headaches or migraines is to determine the precise triggers or contributing variables. Stress, tension, hormone fluctuations, food, and surroundings may all be these triggers.

Use Immediate Relief: EFT tapping is a quick pain-relieving technique that may be used while suffering from a headache or migraine. Verbalize expressions of relief and relaxation while you concentrate on tapping on acupressure points on the head, forehead, and temples.

Handle Stress and Tension: Headaches and migraines are frequently brought on by stress and tension. To promote relaxation and lessen headache symptoms, use EFT tapping to address and release tension and stress in the body.

Target Particular Symptoms: Customize your tapping scripts to specifically address headache or migraine symptoms including throbbing pain, light or sound sensitivity, nausea, or dizziness. Tap to encourage alleviation while providing a detailed description of the experiences.

Examine Emotional Elements: Stress, worry, and emotional discomfort are a few examples of the emotional factors that might have an impact on headaches and migraines. For increased relaxation and pain relief, use EFT tapping to examine and release any emotional discomfort linked to headache symptoms.

Practice Prevention: To avoid headaches and migraines, include consistent EFT tapping into your daily schedule. Tap to release repressed emotions, encourage calmness, and strengthen your resistance to future triggers.

You may lessen the frequency and intensity of headaches, promote relaxation, and enhance your general quality of life by integrating EFT tapping into your headache treatment plan and treating both the physical and emotional elements of pain.

Easing Muscular Tension

One typical physical indication of stress, bad posture, repeated motions, or physical trauma is muscular tension. Persistent muscle tension can impair general mobility and well-being by causing discomfort, stiffness, and a reduction in range of motion. By encouraging relaxation and releasing emotional stress that has been stored in the muscles, EFT tapping provides a mild yet efficient method of reducing muscle tightness.

EFT can be applied in the following ways to reduce muscle tension:

- Determine Tense Areas: To begin, determine which body parts are tense or uncomfortable. This might apply to your jaw, shoulders, back, neck, or other often tense parts of your muscles.

- Use Body Scanning: Spend a few minutes examining every part of your body, from head to toe, feeling for any tight or uncomfortable spots. For each tight place, use EFT tapping to apply pressure to the corresponding acupressure points while uttering words of relaxation and release.

- Release Emotional Stress: Tightness held in the body and emotional stress are frequently associated with muscular tension. For increased relaxation and relief from the symptoms of muscle tension, use EFT tapping to examine and release any emotional stress or tightness.

- Practice Progressive Relaxation: To improve relaxation and lessen tense muscles, use progressive muscle relaxation techniques with EFT tapping. Begin by tensing and then releasing each muscle group while you confirm sensations of ease and relaxation and tap on acupressure points.

- Take Care of Your Postural Habits: Tense and uncomfortable muscles can be caused by poor posture and repetitive motions. To enhance body awareness and alignment and treat any underlying movement patterns or postural habits that could be causing muscle tension, use EFT tapping.

- Use Self-Care Practices: To maximize the benefits of EFT tapping, include self-care techniques like massage, hot/cold treatment, mild stretching, or hydrotherapy to help relax muscles and increase blood flow.

You may lessen muscular tension, promote relaxation, and enhance general mobility and well-being by integrating EFT tapping into your approach to managing physical and emotional stress in your muscles.

EFT FOR EMOTIONAL WELL-BEING

A person's emotional well-being is an essential component of their overall health and quality of life. It encompasses emotions such as happiness, contentment, and the ability to persevere in the face of the obstacles that life presents. Through the process of addressing underlying emotional difficulties, releasing negative emotions, and fostering good feelings and attitudes, Emotional Freedom Techniques (EFT) provides a powerful and diverse technique for promoting emotional well-being. This in-depth investigation will look into the use of EFT for emotional well-being, including the enhancement of self-esteem and confidence, the healing of previous trauma, and the cultivation of good emotions.

Boosting Self-Esteem and Confidence

When it comes to our emotional well-being, self-esteem and confidence are crucial components. They have a significant impact on how we view ourselves, how we relate to other people, and how we navigate through life. Individuals who have low self-esteem and confidence may experience emotions of inadequacy, self-doubt, and fear of failure, which can have a significant influence on different elements of their day-to-day lives. tapping with EFT is an excellent method for raising self-esteem and confidence. This is accomplished by addressing the underlying beliefs that are related to self-worth and releasing the negative emotions that are associated with it.

To improve one's self-esteem and confidence, EFT may be utilized in the following ways:

Determine Limiting Beliefs: To begin, it is important to determine whether or not you have any limiting beliefs or negative self-talk that contributes to poor self-esteem and confidence. Thoughts like "I'm not good enough," "I'm undeserving of love," and "I'll never succeed" are examples of the kinds of beliefs that might be held by individuals.

Negative self-talk may be challenged and reframed through the use of EFT tapping, which can also be used to combat limiting beliefs. While you are tapping on acupressure points, you should also be verbalizing affirmations of self-acceptance, worthiness, and empowerment.

It is important to address prior experiences since low self-esteem and confidence might be the result of previous experiences of being rejected, criticized, or failing. Through the use of EFT tapping, you may investigate and let go of any emotional suffering that is related to these prior events. This will help you to have more compassion and forgiveness for yourself.

By incorporating visualization methods into your EFT tapping practice, you may see yourself succeeding and accomplishing the goals you have set for yourself. To reinforce positive imagery and affirmations of confidence and competence, tapping may be quite helpful.

Cultivate self-compassion and kindness toward oneself, especially during moments of self-doubt or uncertainty. This is especially important to practice when you are feeling emotionally vulnerable. Self-love, acceptance, and gratitude are all sentiments that may be accessed via the use of EFT tapping.

Increasing your self-esteem and confidence, increasing your level of self-acceptance, and cultivating a greater sense of empowerment and self-assurance are all possible outcomes of incorporating EFT tapping into your daily routine and addressing the underlying beliefs and feelings that are causing you distress.

Healing Past Trauma

A person is said to have experienced past trauma when they have gone through considerable emotional or psychological anguish, which can have long-lasting impacts on their mental and emotional well-being. Deep emotional scars can be left behind by traumatic experiences such as accidents, abuse, grief, or violence, and these wounds can affect many different facets of life. Through the release of emotional discomfort, the resolution of negative beliefs, and the promotion of emotional resilience and healing, EFT tapping provides a method that is both gentle and effective for aiding in the healing process of prior trauma.

Some of the ways that EFT may be utilized to recover from prior trauma are as follows:

Begin by acknowledging the traumatic experience and the influence it has had on your life. This is the first step in the healing process. Your emotional responses to the traumatic experience, such as feelings of fear, anger, grief, or humiliation, should be acknowledged and validated and acknowledged.

Employ Safe Tapping Practices: When practicing EFT tapping, it is important to do so in a setting that is both safe and supportive. You should also allow yourself to feel any emotions that come up without resistance or judgment. To tap on acupressure sites while simultaneously verbalizing affirmations of gratitude and acceptance, you should use techniques that involve mild tapping.

Release Emotional Discomfort: EFT tapping may be used to release the emotional distress that is linked with the trauma, such as emotions of dread, remorse, or shame. It is possible to achieve better emotional healing and resolution by tapping on acupressure points while simultaneously verbalizing affirmations of forgiveness and release during the process.

Addressing Negative Views: An individual may develop negative beliefs about themselves, others, and the world as a result of traumatic experiences. These negative ideas may be challenged and reframed via the use of EFT tapping, and they can be replaced with powerful affirmations, such as safety, resilience, and self-compassion.

If you are having difficulty healing from prior trauma on your own, it is recommended that you seek treatment from a skilled mental health professional who is trained in trauma therapy. EFT tapping can be used as a complimentary technique with other therapies that are supported by research, such as cognitive-behavioral therapy (CBT) or eye movement desensitization and reprocessing (EMDR) (EMDR).

You may increase emotional resilience, relieve emotional pain, and regain a sense of safety and empowerment in your life by adding EFT tapping into your trauma healing path, and addressing underlying emotions and beliefs. This will allow you to recover your life.

Cultivating Positive Emotions

Joy, appreciation, love, and contentment are examples of positive emotions that play an important part in emotional well-being. These feelings contribute to increased resilience, pleasure, and overall happiness. Enhancing one's emotional well-being, increasing one's resilience to stress, and promoting a higher feeling of fulfillment and life satisfaction can be accomplished through the cultivation of positive emotions through activities such as EFT tapping.

To promote happy emotions, EFT may be utilized in a variety of ways, including the following:

- Concentrate on Gratitude: Whether it's your well-being, connections with others, accomplishments, or small joys in life, begin by concentrating on the things you have to be thankful for. To truly feel the pleasure and wealth in your life, use EFT tapping to access sentiments of appreciation and gratitude.

- Develop a loving-kindness practice by being loving, compassionate, and kind to both yourself and other people. By using EFT tapping to access feelings of acceptance, forgiveness, and self-love, you may increase your capacity for compassion and strengthen your bonds with other people.

- Imagine Success: Envision yourself accomplishing your objectives and leading the life of your desires. By utilizing EFT tapping, you may access emotions of enthusiasm, empowerment, and confidence that will enable you to completely accept your possibilities and potential.

- Take Care of Yourself: Make time for self-care activities that make you happy and fulfilled. These might include interacting with loved ones, going on a nature walk, or pursuing hobbies and interests. To completely recharge and restore your energy, use EFT tapping to access sensations of calm, renewal, and relaxation.

- Practice Mindfulness: To properly enjoy and recognize the beauty and richness of life, cultivate mindfulness and present-moment awareness. Utilize EFT tapping to access sensations of calm, awareness, and present so that you may give your whole attention to every experience and moment.

You may improve emotional well-being, boost stress resilience, and feel more pleasure, fullness, and satisfaction in your life by adding EFT tapping into your daily routine, and concentrating on nurturing positive emotions.

PART III: ADVANCED TECHNIQUES AND APPLICATIONS

EFT FOR PEAK PERFORMANCE

When people are at their most productive, creative, and effective in the things they do, they are said to be performing at their peak. Peak success in sports, public speaking, academics, and professional endeavors necessitates a trifecta of mental, emotional, and physical preparedness. By addressing underlying emotional obstacles, lowering performance anxiety, and encouraging a state of flow and attention, Emotional Freedom Techniques (EFT) offer a potent tool for improving peak performance. This in-depth investigation will focus on using EFT to achieve peak performance, which includes boosting athletic performance, honing public speaking abilities, and succeeding in academic and professional endeavors.

Enhancing Sports Performance

Several aspects can affect a person's success in sports, including their physical fitness, technical competence, and mental resistance. Individuals' athletic performance can be greatly influenced by a variety of emotional elements, including performance anxiety, self-doubt, and fear of failing. When it comes to overcoming these emotional obstacles and improving their performance on the field or court, EFT tapping is a useful technique that athletes may incorporate into their routines.

The following are some of the ways that EFT may be utilized to improve athletic performance:

Handle Performance Anxiety: Tension, distraction, and a decline in confidence are classic symptoms of performance anxiety, which is a problem for athletes. To improve attention and relaxation during competition, use EFT tapping to address and release anxiety-related feelings including dread, worry, and self-doubt.

Visualize Success: To help you see yourself reaching your maximum potential when using EFT tapping, including visualization methods in your practice. To prepare your mind for optimal performance, use tapping to reaffirm confident, skillful, and successful visions and affirmations.

Let Go of Past Failures: Mental obstacles that impede athletic performance might be caused by past setbacks or failures. To increase resilience and confidence in the present, use EFT tapping to address and release any emotional pain related to past failures.

Cultivate Mind-Body Awareness: As you exercise and compete, become more conscious of your body's signals. By using EFT tapping to access sensations of calm, power, and concentration, you may completely utilize your physical capabilities and provide your best effort.

Handle Your Pre-Game Nerves: Although some level of anxiety is normal during competition, too much anxiety can negatively impact performance. To reduce nervousness before a game, use EFT tapping. Tap on acupressure points and speak calm, confident, and prepared affirmations aloud.

Through the integration of EFT tapping into their training program and the resolution of emotional blockages, athletes may enhance their athletic performance, build resilience, and realize their maximum potential.

Improving Public Speaking Skills

The ability to communicate effectively in front of an audience is a crucial talent that is necessary for success in many aspects of life, including the professional world, education, and personal growth. One of the most prevalent challenges, however, is the fear of public speaking, which may damage confidence and make it more difficult to communicate effectively. The use of EFT tapping is a strong method that may be utilized to overcome anxiety associated with public speaking, boost confidence, and facilitate the delivery of captivating presentations with more ease.

There are a few different ways that EFT may be utilized to improve one's ability to speak in public:

Handle Your Dread of Public Speaking: A common cause of worry about public speaking is a deep-seated fear of being judged, rejected, or failing. To overcome and let go of these anxieties and experience more comfort and confidence when speaking in front of others, use EFT tapping.

Boost Your Confidence: Speaking in public effectively requires confidence. To feel competent, confident, and self-assured, use

EFT tapping. This will empower you to take charge and talk with authority and conviction.

Visualize Success: Make use of visualization techniques to put oneself in the position of making confident, easy-going presentations. By training your mind for optimal performance, use EFT tapping to reinforce affirmations of success and positive visions.

Practice Relaxation Techniques: To lessen anxiety and encourage a state of peace and attention before speaking engagements, incorporate mindfulness meditation, progressive muscle relaxation, and deep breathing into your EFT tapping practice.

Get Ready and Practice: Speaking in public effectively requires preparation. As you prepare and practice your presentations, use EFT tapping to access feelings of clarity, focus, and preparedness. This will help you feel confident and well-prepared.

Through the integration of EFT tapping into their public speaking training and preparation, people may surmount performance anxiety, boost their self-assurance, and effortlessly and authentically make powerful presentations.

Excelling in Academic and Professional Pursuits

To succeed in school and the workplace, one has to have a certain set of skills, knowledge, and mentality. Procrastination, self-doubt, and stress are examples of emotional variables that might impair one's performance in school and at work. To overcome these emotional obstacles, boost motivation and concentrate, and succeed in both scholastic and professional efforts, EFT tapping is a useful tool.

Using EFT can help you succeed in your academic and professional endeavors in the following ways:

Handle Test Anxiety: Students frequently struggle with test anxiety, which can negatively impact their performance on quizzes and evaluations. To improve attention, clarity, and recall during tests, use EFT tapping to address and release test-related anxiety.

Boost Productivity and Enthusiasm: Academic and professional performance might be hampered by procrastination and a lack of motivation. By using EFT tapping to access feelings of drive, determination, and motivation, you may overcome procrastination and move toward your goals.

Overcome Imposter Syndrome: Imposter syndrome is a condition in which people have self-doubt and worry about being revealed as scammers. To acknowledge and appreciate your abilities and successes, use EFT tapping to address and release emotions of unworthiness and self-doubt.

Improve Concentration and Focus: Both academic and professional success depends on concentration and focus. By using EFT tapping to access sensations of alertness, clarity, and attention, you may maintain your focus and engagement during work or study periods.

Handle Performance Pressure: Stress and anxiety can be brought on by the pressure to do well in school or at work. Increased calmness, self-assurance, and resilience in high-pressure circumstances can be achieved by using EFT tapping to address and release performance-related stress.

People may improve attention and motivation, lessen stress and anxiety, and succeed in their academic and professional endeavors by implementing EFT tapping into their study and work routines, and addressing emotional blockages.

EFT FOR RELATIONSHIPS

The foundation of the human experience is relationships, which have an impact on our general well-being, pleasure, and contentment. Healthy relationships are based on trust, communication, and emotional connection, whether they be with romantic partners, family, friends, or coworkers. Emotional Freedom Techniques (EFT) are a potent and successful method for mending relationship scars, resolving underlying emotional blockages, and fortifying ties. This thorough investigation will focus on the use of EFT in relationships, including enhancing ties, mending relationship scars, and enhancing communication.

Improving Communication

Good communication enables people to understand and sympathize with others, as well as to communicate their needs, feelings, and limits in healthy and happy relationships. Relationship quality can be negatively impacted by poor communication, which can result in miscommunication, disputes, and animosity. EFT tapping is a useful technique for enhancing communication since it helps to overcome emotional obstacles, increase empathy, and encourage candid and open discussion.

The following are some methods that EFT may be applied to enhance interpersonal communication:

Determine Communication Patterns: To begin, determine the communication patterns that lead to miscommunications or disputes in the partnership. A few examples of this may be avoiding awkward situations, acting passive-aggressively, or not actively listening.

Address Emotional Obstacles: Ineffective communication might be impeded by emotional barriers like fear, insecurity, or traumatic experiences in the past. To overcome these emotional obstacles and enable more emotional openness, vulnerability, and connection in conversation, use EFT tapping.

Engage in Active Listening: Good communication requires the fundamental ability of active listening. By using EFT tapping to access feelings of presence, empathy, and understanding, you may validate other people's viewpoints and completely listen to them without being defensive or judgmental.

Express Needs and Limits: To access feelings of self-awareness and assertiveness, use EFT tapping. This will enable you to respectfully communicate your needs, feelings, and boundaries. Instead of placing blame or offering criticism on other people, use "I" statements and concentrate on sharing your own experience.

Constructive Conflict Resolution: Although disagreements will inevitably arise in relationships, how they are settled may either improve or worsen the bond between the parties. By using EFT tapping to access emotions of peace, empathy, and cooperation, you can facilitate productive conversation and conflict resolution.

People may enhance their communication skills, develop greater empathy, and cultivate a deeper level of connection and understanding in their relationships by implementing EFT tapping into their communication practices, and addressing emotional blockages.

Healing Relationship Wounds

Relationship wounds are psychological traumas or injuries that arise in the context of a relationship and are frequently brought on by betrayal, rejection, or abandonment experiences. Relationship patterns characterized by conflict and separation might result from these scars, which can obstruct intimacy and trust. By addressing underlying emotions, encouraging forgiveness and acceptance, and promoting healing and reconciliation, EFT tapping provides a compassionate and effective method for treating relationship scars.

EFT can be applied in the following ways to mend relationship wounds:

- Recognize the Wound: To begin, acknowledge the existence of relationship wounds and how they affect the partnership. Give yourself permission to completely process and recognize your suffering by acknowledging and validating your own experiences and feelings connected to the wound.

- Address Emotional Pain: Anger, sadness, or grief are common emotional pains that accompany relationship traumas. To facilitate more emotional healing and wound closure, use EFT tapping to address and release these feelings.

- Practice Forgiveness: Letting go of grudges and moving forward with more empathy and understanding are made possible by forgiveness, which is a crucial step in mending relationship wounds. EFT tapping can help you access emotions of empathy, compassion, and forgiveness so you can let go of grudges and resentments.

- Rebuild Trust: Following a relationship breakup, trust must be rebuilt with persistence, openness, and consistency. By using EFT tapping to access feelings of honesty, dependability, and trustworthiness, you may show that you are a trustworthy person by your words and deeds.

- Seek Professional Support: If you're having trouble mending the scars in your relationships, you might want to think about getting help from a licensed therapist or counselor who specializes in trauma recovery or couples therapy. In addition to other evidence-based therapies, EFT tapping can be utilized as a supplemental strategy to encourage relationship repair and reconciliation.

People may facilitate forgiveness, healing, and reconciliation in their relationships and increase intimacy, trust, and connection by addressing emotional blockages and integrating EFT into their recovery path.

Strengthening Bonds

Good and satisfying relationships are built on strong emotional ties that provide people with a sense of safety, support, and community. However, sustaining close relationships calls for constant work and consideration of each person's emotional requirements. By encouraging emotional connection, intimacy, and the development of empathy and mutual understanding, EFT tapping is a useful technique for fortifying relationships.

The following are some strategies for using EFT to improve relationship bonds:

Develop Emotional Connection: Solid relationships are built on emotional connections. By using EFT tapping to access emotions of warmth, tenderness, and empathy, you may establish a stronger emotional connection with your partner or other loved one.

Show Your Appreciation and Gratitude: By recognizing and appreciating the contributions made by each member of the relationship, showing your appreciation and gratitude helps to build relationships between people. By using EFT tapping to access sentiments of appreciation and gratitude, you may communicate to your partner or other loved one your sincere gratitude and acknowledgment.

Share Your Vulnerability: Relationship closeness and trust are developed by vulnerability. To communicate your concerns, insecurities, and goals with a spouse or loved one in a secure and encouraging setting, use EFT tapping to access feelings of vulnerability.

Develop Your Empathy: Empathy is the capacity to comprehend and experience another person's feelings. To affirm and sympathize with your partner's or loved one's experiences and emotions, use EFT tapping to access feelings of empathy and compassion.

Establish Rituals of Connection: Rituals of connection are heartfelt customs or practices that bolster links and foster shared experiences in interpersonal relationships. By using EFT tapping to access sensations of joy and connection, you may enable yourself to establish and maintain rituals of connection that deepen your relationship.

People may build stronger ties, more intimate relationships, and deeper, more satisfying ones with their spouses, family, and friends by implementing EFT tapping into their relationship practices, and encouraging emotional connection.

PART IV: INTEGRATING EFT TAPPING INTO DAILY LIFE

CREATING PERSONALIZED TAPPING SCRIPTS

When it comes to the use of Emotional Freedom Techniques, personalized tapping scripts are extremely effective instruments (EFT). By combining the tapping on acupressure points with affirmations or phrases that are linked to the situation at hand, they make it possible for individuals to address specific emotional difficulties, traumas, or ambitions and achieve their desired outcomes. When it comes to crafting successful tailored tapping scripts, it is necessary to first identify the needs of the individual, then modify the script so that it addresses those needs, and last, improve the EFT session so that it yields the best possible outcomes. This in-depth investigation will go into the process of producing individualized tapping scripts, which includes the creation of powerful affirmations, the customization of scripts to specific requirements, and the enhancement of EFT sessions.

Crafting Effective Affirmations

Affirmations are utterances that are positive or affirmations of outcomes that are wanted. They are utilized during EFT tapping to establish and strengthen positive thoughts and intentions. Choosing words and phrases that resonate with the individual's goals, values, and emotional experiences is an important step in the process of crafting successful affirmations. Effective affirmations are those that are favorable, written in the present tense, and emotionally resonant. This enables them to bring about changes in thinking patterns and beliefs.

To develop successful affirmations for individualized tapping scripts, the following recommendations are provided:

Be Upbeat: It's important to structure affirmations in a way that gives them strength and positivity. Focus on the experiences and accomplishments you do want to have, rather than the things you don't desire. For instance, state "I am confident and capable of reaching my goals" rather than "I am not frightened of failing."

Employ the Present Tense: When stating affirmations, it is best to do so as though the intended result has already been attained. This contributes to the affirmation's sense of urgency and conviction. Say, for instance, "I am conquering my worries with ease and elegance," rather than "I shall overcome my fears."

Be Precise: Affirmations have to be targeted toward the intended result or experience and ought to be specific. Be specific about what you wish to materialize instead of making generic or ambiguous claims. Say, for instance, "I am enjoying joy and satisfaction in my life every day," as opposed to "I am happy."

Employ Emotional Language: Affirmations ought to arouse sentiments of positivity and connection to the intended result. Make use of words and phrases that inspire and motivate you, and that emotionally connect with you. For instance, state "I am thriving and flourishing in every area of my life" rather than "I am succeeding."

Make Them Credible: The person making the affirmation should find it credible and attainable. Select affirmations that are consistent with your values, beliefs, and degree of change preparedness at the moment. Beginning with affirmations that are easy for you to believe in, go on to more difficult ones as your self-assurance and self-belief grow.

People may build customized tapping scripts that reinforce good beliefs and intentions and result in transformative transformations in thinking patterns and behaviors by generating powerful affirmations that are positive, explicit, emotionally resonant, and convincing.

Tailoring Scripts to Specific Needs

Tapping scripts that are specifically designed to address an individual's emotional needs, issues, or aspirations are the most successful ones. This entails figuring out which underlying emotional problems or beliefs are causing the issue, picking suitable tapping locations, and finding affirmations that speak to the person's experience. Individuals may address their struggles and experiences by having scripts tailored to their requirements, which produces more significant and long-lasting outcomes.

To customize scripts for particular requirements, follow these steps:

Determine the Issue: To begin using EFT tapping to address a specific emotional issue, obstacle, or goal, identify it first. This might be anything from self-doubt and limiting beliefs to worry and anxiety.

Examine Underlying Emotions: Learn more about the underlying feelings and ideas that are fueling the issue. Discover the underlying reasons for your emotional difficulties via writing, reflection, or guided visualization.

Pick Tapping Points: Decide which tapping points are most pertinent to the problem you are trying to solve. Points like the eyebrow, side of the eye, chin, collarbone, underarm, under nose, and top of the head may be among them.

Create Affirmations: Create affirmations that speak directly to the underlying feelings and ideas that you previously recognized. Utilize the criteria for creating powerful affirmations to construct sentences that emotionally connect with you and support your goals.

Sequence Tapping Points: As you repeat the affirmations, decide which order to tap on the acupressure points. Begin from the side of the hand, which is the karate chop point. Proceed logically through the remaining locations, concluding with the top of the head.

Repeat and Fine-tune: While keeping your attention on the problem you are trying to solve, repeat the tapping script a few times. Keep an eye out for any changes in your feelings, ideas, or bodily experiences, and adjust the script as necessary to address the underlying problems in more detail.

Through customization of tapping scripts to individual requirements and resolution of underlying emotional problems or beliefs, people can undergo more profound healing and life change, resulting in improved emotional health and personal development.

Enhancing EFT Sessions

Improving EFT sessions entails adding new methods, instruments, or routines to maximize the tapping process' efficacy. To enhance attention, induce deeper states of relaxation, and facilitate emotional integration and healing, this may involve combining EFT tapping with other mind-body practices including breathing exercises, mindfulness, and visualization. Improving EFT sessions enables people to tailor their tapping technique to their requirements and preferences, producing more significant and long-lasting outcomes.

The following are some ideas to improve EFT sessions:

- Combine with Mindfulness: During your EFT tapping sessions, use mindfulness exercises like body scanning, attentive awareness, or deep breathing. This aids in stress reduction, relaxation, and emotional integration in addition to raising awareness of the current moment.

- Use Visualization: To see yourself achieving your desired result or objective, combine EFT tapping with visualization techniques. To conjure up images in your mind of achievement and empowerment, use sensory details, strong imagery, and empowering statements.

- During EFT tapping, practice gradual relaxation by using strategies to reduce tension and encourage relaxation throughout the body. To facilitate deeper relaxation and integration, begin by tensing and then releasing each muscle group while tapping on the acupressure points.

- Include Breathwork: During EFT tapping, use breathwork techniques like diaphragmatic breathing or alternate nostril breathing to control your breathing, encourage relaxation, and maintain emotional equilibrium. To increase the efficiency of the tapping technique, concentrate on taking calm, deep breaths while tapping on the acupressure points.

- Establish Clear Intentions: Prioritize what you want to accomplish or bring into your life when setting clear intentions or objectives for your EFT tapping sessions. To program your subconscious mind for success and transformation, use declarations of intention or affirmations.

- Practice Gratitude: During EFT tapping sessions, cultivate sentiments of appreciation and gratitude by concentrating on the things you have in your life for which you are thankful. To truly appreciate the benefits in your life, use tapping to access feelings of gratitude, pleasure, and abundance.

Through the incorporation of supplementary methods, tools, or practices into EFT sessions, individuals may enhance their tapping practice, promote relaxation and emotional integration, and achieve more significant and enduring outcomes in their personal growth and healing process.

MAINTAINING PROGRESS AND LONG-TERM SUCCESS

When it comes to Emotional Freedom Techniques (EFT), there is more to it than simply resolving immediate problems or difficulties to maintain development and achieve long-term success. It is necessary to maintain a level of devotion and resilience, as well as to include EFT into everyday routines, to effectively promote continuous growth and well-being. We will examine ways to overcome plateaus, establish resilience, and incorporate EFT into everyday routines to ensure continuous growth and long-term success. This full investigation will take place to bring about these outcomes.

Overcoming Plateaus

Plateaus are a regular occurrence in any path of personal development, including the practice of EFT. They take place when development comes to a halt, and individuals may experience feelings of being stuck or stagnant in their journey of healing or growing. Accomplishing success after reaching a plateau calls for patience, perseverance, and a willingness to investigate alternative methods or points of view.

To break through plateaus in EFT practice, the following tactics might be utilized:

- Examine Underlying Issues: If deeper underlying issues are present and haven't been properly addressed, plateaus may occasionally result. To investigate any unresolved feelings, thoughts, or traumas that could be causing the plateau, use EFT tapping.

- Attempt Various Methods: Don't be scared to try a different tapping script or strategy if the one you're using isn't yielding the intended results. Try out various affirmations, tapping sequences, and mindfulness exercises to determine what suits you the best.

- Seek Assistance: For direction and help, get in touch with a licensed EFT practitioner or therapist. To assist you in overcoming obstacles and advancing farther, they might provide you with advice, criticism, and customized tapping scripts.

- Develop Self-Compassion: Show yourself kindness and compassion when you reach a standstill. Recognize that obstacles are a normal part of the path and that healing and progress are nonlinear processes. Use self-compassion and self-care techniques to support oneself throughout trying situations.

- Remain Consistent: Overcoming plateaus requires consistency. Even if you feel like your development is stalling or going slowly, keep up your daily EFT tapping practice.

Have faith in the procedure and remain dedicated to your path of recovery and development.

You may overcome plateaus and keep moving closer to your objectives by taking the initiative, asking for help when you need it, and practicing EFT consistently.

Building Resilience

One's resilience may be defined as the capacity to recover quickly from adversity, to deal with obstacles, and to adjust to new circumstances. Establishing a resilient mindset is necessary to sustain the forward movement and achieve success with EFT over the long run. People can negotiate the ups and downs of life with more ease and resilience as a result of this development.

When it comes to EFT practice, the following are some techniques to improve resilience:

Develop Mindfulness: Techniques like body scanning, deep breathing, and meditation can help develop resilience and present-moment awareness. To enhance emotional balance, lower stress levels, and raise self-awareness, incorporate mindfulness into your EFT practice.

Practice Gratitude: Develop an attitude of thankfulness and appreciation for all of life's blessings. To promote resilience and happiness, try keeping a gratitude notebook or adding appreciation comments to your EFT tapping sessions.

Develop Coping Skills: To handle stress, anxiety, or difficult emotions, recognize and cultivate appropriate coping mechanisms. This might involve methods like deep breathing exercises, creative problem-solving, or enlisting the help of others.

Create a Support System: Assemble a network of friends, family, or other EFT practitioners who are there to offer you support, understanding, and empathy when things become tough. Having a robust support system is crucial for resilience and overall wellbeing.

Embrace a Growth Mentality: Develop a growth mindset by considering obstacles and failures as chances for improvement. Be open-minded, curious, and eager to absorb new information from your EFT practice.

Through the practice of mindfulness, gratitude, coping skill development, support network building, and growth mindset adoption, you may strengthen your resilience and achieve success in both your EFT practice and your life.

Integrating EFT into Daily Routine

Achieving long-term success and sustaining development require incorporating EFT into everyday practices. By ensuring that EFT becomes a routine part of your life, regular practice helps you maintain your continuous healing, development, and wellbeing.

The following are some methods for incorporating EFT into your everyday schedule:

Set Aside Dedicated Time: Plan a consistent period for practicing EFT tapping every day. This may occur when you wake up in the morning, at various points during the day, or right before bed. To form a habit, one must be consistent.

Include EFT in Daily Activities: Include EFT tapping in routine activities like writing, exercise, and meditation. For instance, as part of your daily practice, you might incorporate affirmations or deep breathing exercises with tapping.

Employ Trigger Spots: Throughout the day, mark points that serve as a reminder to practice EFT tapping. This could occur during certain tasks like driving or standing in line, or it could happen when you're stressed, anxious, or experiencing unpleasant feelings.

Make Rituals: To enhance the enjoyment and significance of your EFT practice, create rituals or routines around it. To establish a feeling of sanctity and attention before each tapping session, light a candle, play soothing music, or make an intention.

Monitor Your Progress: Use a monitoring tool or keep a notebook to record your EFT sessions and advancement. To track your development and pinpoint areas that require more research, keep track of any changes you see in your ideas, emotions, or actions over time.

You may encourage continuous healing, growth, and well-being by incorporating EFT into your daily routine and making tapping a natural and seamless part of your life.

CONCLUSION

We have been through the many uses, methods, and significant ramifications of Emotional Freedom Techniques (EFT) tapping treatment for personal development, healing, and change. Let's consider the future of EFT tapping therapy, changing practices, and how people might continue their journey with EFT to support continuous improvement and long-term success as we draw to a close this thorough examination.

The Future of EFT Tapping Therapy

With increasing acceptance and acknowledgment in alternative and conventional medicine, EFT tapping treatment has a bright future ahead of it. EFT is expected to be incorporated into traditional treatment procedures more and more as studies verify its efficacy and our understanding of its mechanics grows. Furthermore, those looking for healing and personal development will probably have easier access to EFT because of technological and accessibility developments.

Furthermore, EFT tapping treatment may be essential in treating the expanding epidemic of stress, anxiety, and trauma-related problems as mental health awareness continues to develop internationally. It is a useful tool for people of all ages and backgrounds who want to improve their general well-being and find relief from emotional discomfort because of its non-invasiveness, simplicity of use, and adaptability.

Furthermore, EFT tapping treatment may provide a way for people to develop resilience, empathy, and compassion, enabling greater communal healing and social change, as society continues to struggle with difficult issues like societal injustice, environmental degradation, and global disasters.

Evolving Practices

The methods around the implementation of EFT tapping treatment are evolving along with our understanding of the technique. The discipline may innovate by combining EFT with other therapeutic modalities, such as somatic experiencing, mindfulness-based therapies, and cognitive-behavioral therapy (CBT), to create synergistic methods that address the complexity of human experience.

Furthermore, technological developments might result in the creation of virtual reality experiences, applications, and digital platforms that support self-guided EFT sessions, provide individualized coaching, and provide users access to a worldwide community of practitioners and enthusiasts. These developments might democratize access to EFT tapping therapy, enabling people in underprivileged or distant locations to get treatment and take control of their emotional health.

Moreover, further investigation may reveal fresh perspectives on the fundamental workings of EFT, clarifying its impacts on the neurological system, the brain, and the stress response. This expanded comprehension might help with the creation of focused therapies for certain groups or situations, improving results and broadening the range of uses for EFT.

Continuing Your Journey with EFT

When starting an EFT tapping treatment journey or looking to advance their practice, there are a few important factors to keep in mind to stay on track and succeed in the long run:

1. Consistency: To benefit from EFT tapping treatment, consistency is essential. Over time, developing a consistent tapping routine—daily, weekly, or as needed—can support resilience development, emotional well-being, and reinforcement of beneficial changes.

2. Self-Reflection: Give your EFT tapping therapy experiences some thought, and record

any changes in your feelings, ideas, or actions. Maintaining a diary may help you become more self-aware and improve by helping you keep track of your accomplishments, revelations, and potential study topics.

3. Continuing Education: Attend conferences, seminars, or online courses, interact with reliable sources and professionals, and stay up to date on advancements in the field of EFT tapping treatment. By expanding your arsenal, learning new ways to practice, and deepening your grasp of EFT principles and practices, continuing education may help.

4. Seeking Support: When necessary, don't be afraid to ask for help from mentors, support

groups, or certified EFT practitioners. Expert advice may offer tailored perspectives, constructive criticism, and responsibility, boosting your advancement and resolving any difficulties or roadblocks in the process.

5. Including EFT in Daily Routine: Include EFT tapping treatment in your regular activities by combining it with mindfulness exercises, physical activity, or self-care routines. Regular integration can support general well-being, stress management, and the reinforcement of healthy behaviors in your day-to-day activities.

To sum up, tapping therapy using Emotional Freedom Techniques (EFT) provides a deep and adaptable method for healing, personal development, and transformation. EFT enables people to manage emotional difficulties, let go of limiting beliefs, and develop more resilience and well-being through a mild yet effective blend of acupressure tapping and affirmations.

Looking ahead, we see a world in which EFT tapping treatment is well known and included in traditional healthcare, education, and personal growth. EFT can completely transform how we approach mental health and emotional well-being via further study, innovation, and activism, giving people all around the world hope and healing.

Remember that change is a lifetime process and that every step you take on your EFT journey is evidence of your bravery, resiliency, and dedication to your development and healing. Accept the opportunities that EFT tapping treatment presents, have faith in your natural ability to transform, and know that you have support along the way as you strive for more wholeness, vigor, and joy.